SPORTS ALL-STARS

LINDSEY VONN

Eric Braun

Lerner Publications ◆ Minneapolis

Lerner Publications Company
A division of Lerner Publishing Group, Inc.
241 First Avenue North
Minneapolis, MN 55401 USA

For reading levels and more information, look up this title at www.lernerbooks.com.

Main body text set in Albany Std 15/22. Typeface provided by Agfa.

Library of Congress Cataloging-in-Publication Data

Names: Braun, Eric, 1971–
Title: Lindsey Vonn / Eric Braun.
Description: Minneapolis : Lerner Publications, [2017] | Includes bibliographical
    references and index.
Identifiers: LCCN 2016025652 (print) | LCCN 2016027312 (ebook) | ISBN
    9781512425802 (lb : alk. paper) | ISBN 9781512431209 (pb : alk. paper) | ISBN
    9781512428254 (eb pdf)
Subjects: LCSH: Vonn, Lindsey—Juvenile literature. | Skiers—United States—
    Biography—Juvenile literature.
Classification: LCC GV854.2.V66 B73 2017 (print) | LCC GV854.2.V66 (ebook) |
    DDC 796.93092 [B] —dc23

LC record available at https://lccn.loc.gov/2016025652

Manufactured in the United States of America
1-41348-23292-8/29/2016

CONTENTS

Lindsey Vonn
soars downhill at
the Lake Louise
World Cup 2015.

Lake Louise in Alberta, Canada, had been good to Lindsey Vonn. Twice before at the **Alpine Ski World Cup** competition held at the resort, she had recorded a **hat trick**—a victory in three events. In December 2015, she returned to Lake Louise for the World Cup. Only this time, the stakes felt a little higher.

Vonn had already been an Olympic skiing champion. And with 67 career wins, she already held the record for most World Cup victories by a female skier. With these accomplishments behind her, why was Vonn nervous?

Vonn wins the women's super-G race at Lake Louise.

She had missed the Lake Louise contest the past two years due to knee injuries. She even had to skip the Winter Olympics in 2014—a huge disappointment for Vonn and her fans. For a long time, Vonn had been the best women's skier in the world. Could she return to form?

Vonn answered that question quickly. At Lake Louise in 2015, she won the first two races she competed in, both **downhill** events. Her third race was the super giant **slalom**, or **super-G**. Compared to other slalom events, the super-G focuses more on speed. The **gates** that skiers pass are set farther apart. This allows skiers to go faster. And *faster* is how Vonn likes to ski.

It didn't take long for Vonn to remind the Lake Louise spectators what she could do on a super-G course. She launched out of the starting gate and attacked the course. She didn't just win the event. She dominated it. She finished in 1 minute, 19.79 seconds. Her time was 1.32 seconds faster than the next best skier—a huge margin of victory.

The three wins at Lake Louise gave Vonn 70 World Cup wins for her career. What's more, 18 of these victories were at Lake Louise, a place many refer to as Lake Lindsey.

Vonn poses with second-place winner Austrian Tamara Tippler (left) and third-place winner Austrian Cornelia Huetter (right) after the 2015 Lake Louise women's super-G race.

CHILDHOOD IN THE SNOW

Vonn began skiing at Buck Hill in Minnesota.

If you look at Buck Hill in Burnsville, Minnesota, you might not think of world-class skiers. Even *hill* seems too big of a word when you compare it to the mountains that host World Cup events. But that is where Vonn got her start.

She took up skiing at the age of three and loved it. Even then, it was clear that she was talented. Her father and grandfather were ski racers. By the age of seven, she was racing too. But she wasn't racing kids her age. She was too good. Instead, she was beating older kids.

Vonn's father, Alan Kildow (left), is a former competitive skier.

"That was not the greatest way to make new friends," she recalled. "I would finish a race and all the 14-year-olds at the bottom would be crying because a 10-year-old had beaten them." Even then, Lindsey thought of skiing as something fun. It wasn't going to be her whole life.

Then, in 1994, Lindsey met one of her heroes. Picabo Street was an Olympic medalist in downhill skiing. She came to Minnesota for a ski show. Lindsey got to see Street's 1994 Olympic silver medal and her World Cup downhill trophy. The meeting changed Lindsey's mind about skiing just for fun. She wanted to compete in the Olympics.

Picabo Street won the gold medal for the women's super-G race in the 1998 Winter Olympics.

Lindsey developed her skills in the mountains of Vail, Colorado.

When Lindsey was 11, her family moved to Vail, Colorado. There were real mountains there. She got even better at skiing and began winning events all around the world.

At the age of 17, Lindsey reached her goal. She qualified for the 2002 Olympics in Salt Lake City, Utah. She placed sixth in the **combined event**. It was the best finish by an American woman skier that year. Two years later, in December 2004, Lindsey won her first World Cup—at Lake Louise.

Vonn trained hard to become a champion.

Early in her career, Vonn was a very good skier. But she wasn't *great*. She wasn't the best.

Who was the best? On the US Ski Team, it was Vonn's teammate, Julia Mancuso. The two skiers were friends—and also rivals. But in those years, Vonn couldn't ski out of Mancuso's shadow. Then they took a bike ride together that changed everything.

Vonn and Julia Mancuso (right) were close friends and rivals on the US Ski Team.

Mancuso invited Vonn to her family's Lake Tahoe home. During the visit, Mancuso and her dad took Vonn on a bike ride along the mountain roads. Though Vonn was a professional athlete, she couldn't keep up with the other two. She soon found herself five miles behind.

An intense bike ride through the Lake Tahoe mountains inspired Vonn to kick her training into high gear.

"I felt like a fool," Vonn later said. How could she expect to be the best if Mancuso was in such better shape? Vonn realized she would have to work very hard if she wanted to beat her friend.

Vonn began working out eight hours a day, six days a week. Slowly, her endurance increased. She had built a superpowerful lower body. Before long, it showed on the slopes. She was the top dog on the US Ski Team.

Vonn works on balance and strength training to stay at the top of her game.

Vonn had to take a break from competing after her 2013 knee injury required surgery.

The only thing that keeps Vonn from working out is injury. Unfortunately, she has been injured several times. That's partly because Vonn's skiing style is all out. She ferociously attacks every course. This style has helped her win two Olympic medals and, with six more wins since her 2015 victory at Lake

Vonn's dog Leo had a hurt knee in 2014 too! While Vonn recovered from her knee surgery, Leo stayed by her side and gave her support.

Louise, 76 World Cup races.

But it has also gotten her hurt. In her career, she has torn knee **ligaments** three times. Twice she has had serious knee surgeries. She has broken a leg twice and broken an ankle once.

Vonn finds it hard to take a break while her body heals. So she finds ways to keep exercising even when hurt. She has been seen doing upside-down sit-ups hanging from a bar—with her foot in a cast.

Vonn used crutches when she walked the runway at a 2014 charity event.

Vonn is a fast, aggressive skier.

Because of her injuries, Vonn works extra hard to stay healthy and is dedicated to keeping at the top of her game. In fact, she's so dedicated that she keeps her intense workout routines secret.

She doesn't want anyone to copy what she's doing.

"I am motivated by the idea that no one else is doing these crazy things," she said when describing her workout schedule. Vonn works out all the time. She has been known to do push-ups in the aisle during airplane trips. Her tough workouts help her stay strong and give her confidence that she's stronger than her competitors.

Vonn prefers men's skis. They tend to be heavier and stiffer than women's. "For me, the men's skis are more stable. It's harder to turn, of course, it takes more strength. But I'm able to generate a lot of speed from the turns."

Vonn celebrated in a private party with the girls who graduated from her 2015 Ski Girls Rock program, where she led a special workout session and signed some autographs.

Vonn's lifestyle is about more than just athletics. She wants young women to be as aggressive and confident as she is. That's why she works hard for girls' groups. The Lindsey Vonn Foundation works to empower girls everywhere. Vonn sponsors scholarships to help girls get the best education. Programs such as her summer camp help girls become better athletes and more confident young women.

Vonn also has a passion for fun. As a celebrity athlete, she has made guest appearances on many TV shows, including *Law & Order*, *Project Runway*, and Nickelodeon's *Kids' Choice Sports* awards show. She has even done some modeling. Her face is one of the most recognizable in the world.

Vonn was a guest judge on an episode of *Project Runway*.

In 2005, Vonn's fun side was on display after she won a race in France. Part of her prize was a bouquet of flowers . . . and a cow. Most winners choose to sell the cow. It is usually considered a symbol of victory rather than a prize to take home. But Vonn kept her cow. She named it Olympe and started a family of cows. She has a herd of five. Another time, she was awarded a goat. She named it Laura, after her sister.

Most people might think of these as smelly prizes to get rid of quickly. Vonn saw a chance to try something fun and unusual. Her cows and goat live with farmers in Austria, near where Vonn used to train.

Vonn kept her 2005 prize and named it Olympe.

Roger Federer (*left*) and Vonn played a friendly tennis match on a specially made court on top of a glacier.

In the 2010 Winter Olympics, Vonn crashed during a race and broke her pinkie finger.

Vonn wins so often it's almost routine. The one thing that stops her from winning is injury. When she gets injured, she can't ski—so she can't win.

Late in 2012, she was racking up wins, including a hat trick at Lake Louise. But the following February, she landed awkwardly after a jump and tumbled down the mountain. She tore ligaments in her knee, broke her leg, and had to end her season. After surgery, she worked hard to get back into action. Vonn hit the slopes again in the fall, but she'd come back too soon, and her knee gave out at an event in France. Again, she trained as hard as she could to recover.

As she **rehabbed** her knee, she was forced to skip the 2014 Olympics in Sochi, Russia. Finally, after nearly two years away from the sport, Vonn returned for the 2014–2015 season. She grabbed her 62nd

Vonn's 2015 victory in the downhill race in Italy gave her a tie for the most World Cup victories for a female skier.

World Cup victory in January 2015, tying her for the career record for female skiers. The next day, Vonn took another big step. She won first place in the super-G race and, with that win, became the most successful female skier of all time.

The wins kept coming. In December, she earned her second hat trick at Lake Louise. That brought her career total to an even 70. By February 2016, she was up to 76 career wins. Later that month, she attended an event in Soldeu, Andorra. There was heavy snow and a powerful wind that day. Vonn was leading her event when her ski got caught in soft snow and she lost control. She crashed hard and had to be taken off the hill on a rescue sled.

Vonn was carried off the course after her crash in Soldeu.

"When I was laying there, I knew something bad had happened because I could feel the bone hit bone," she said. Vonn had a **fractured** bone in her knee.

Then, the next day, despite this painful injury, she skied the super-G. Wearing braces on both knees, she nailed the best time of the day. She won the event!

Her joy was short-lived. The next day, her knee was examined again. She actually had a *triple* fracture.

Vonn wore knee braces to compete in the super-G race the day after her crash.

With that news, Vonn made a hard decision. She would not compete the rest of the season.

Of course, that doesn't mean the furious worker is sitting out the season completely. She is training as hard as ever, just as she always does. With 76 victories, Vonn has won more World Cup events than any other woman. But the all-time record is 86, held by Ingemar Stenmark of Sweden. Vonn has her sights set on that number. With her incredible skill and history of recovering from injuries, chances are good that she'll beat it.

All-Star Stats

There are five races in alpine skiing: downhill, super-G, slalom, giant slalom, and combined. Vonn holds the most wins by anyone—man or woman—in downhill and super-G. Those are the two races in which skiers go the fastest.

Downhill Wins

38 Lindsey Vonn, female, USA
36 Annemarie Moser-Pröll, female, Austria
25 Franz Klammer, male, Austria

Super-G Wins

27 Lindsey Vonn, female, USA
24 Hermann Maier, male, Austria
17 Renate Götschl, female, Austria

Source Notes

10   Bill Pennington, "Lindsey Vonn at the Summit," *New York Times Magazine*, February 3, 2010, http://www.nytimes.com/2010/02/07/magazine/07Vonn-t.html?_r=1.

15   Charles Robinson, "Frenemy Lines: Vonn Seals Spot as USA's 'Top Dog,'" *Yahoo! Sports*, February 17, 2010, http://sports.yahoo.com/news/frenemy-lines-vonn-seals-spot-033300172--oly.html.

19   Pennington, "Lindsey Vonn."

19   Associated Press, "Vonn's Secret to Success? Men's Skis," *SFGate*, December 19, 2009, http://www.sfgate.com/sports/article/Vonn-s-secret-to-success-Men-s-skis-3278330.php.

26   Nick Zaccardi, "Lindsey Vonn Details Screams, 'Excruciating Pain' in Season-Ending Crash," *NBC Sports*, April 4, 2016, http://olympics.nbcsports.com/2016/04/04/lindsey-vonn-crash-lara-gut-alpine-skiing/.

Glossary

Alpine Ski World Cup: a yearly competition in which skiers compete in alpine skiing events over a number of meets during the winter. The winners are the male and female skiers with the highest combined points earned from each race.

combined event: a skiing competition involving one run of downhill and two runs of slalom. The winner is the skier with the fastest combined time.

downhill: a ski race in which the gates are the farthest apart of all events and also includes turns, dips, and jumps

fractured: broken or cracked

gates: poles that skiers have to go around in a ski race

hat trick: when a skier wins three races at a single event

ligaments: tough tissue that connects body parts

rehabbed: brought back to a healthy or normal condition after injury or illness

slalom: in skiing, a race over a winding course that is marked by flags

super-G: short for super giant slalom; a ski race in which the gates are farther apart than in slalom or giant slalom, allowing skiers to gain more speed

Further Information

Dann, Sarah. *Lindsey Vonn*. New York: Crabtree, 2014.

Fishman, Jon M. *Mikaela Shiffrin*. Minneapolis: Lerner Publications, 2015.

Lindsey Vonn
http://www.lindseyvonn.com

The Lindsey Vonn Foundation
http://www.lindseyvonnfoundation.org

Nagelhout, Ryan. *Lindsey Vonn*. New York: Gareth Stevens, 2017.

Time for Kids—Alpine Skiing
http://www.timeforkids.com/news/alpine-skiing/137666

Yomtov, Nel. *The Science of a Carve Turn*. Ann Arbor, MI: Cherry Lake, 2016.

Index

Photo Acknowledgments

The images in this book are used with the permission of: GUILLAUME HORCAJUELO/EPA/Newscom, p. 2 (background); © iStockphoto.com/iconeer (gold stars); Eric Bolte/USA Today Sports/Newscom, pp. 4–5; Sergei Belski/USA Today Sports/Newscom, pp. 6, 7; Carlos Gonzalez/Polaris/Newscom, p. 8; AP Photo/Andrew Dampf, p. 9; AP Photo/Luca Bruno, pp. 10, 13; © Jbksox15/Dreamstime.com, p. 11; © JEFF HAYNES/Getty Images, p. 12; © iStockphoto.com/David Safanda, p. 14; AP Photo/Pat Graham, p. 15; © Wally Skalij/Los Angeles Times via Getty Images, p. 16; AP Photo/Brad Barket/Invision, p. 17; © PHOTOMDP/Shutterstock.com, p. 18; Elizabeth Flores/ZUMA Press/Newscom, p. 20; Johns PKI/Splash News/Newscom, p. 21; © OLIVIER MORIN/AFP/Getty Images, p. 22; AP Photo/Alexandra Wey for LINDT, p. 23; David Mavro/ZUMA Press/Newscom, p. 24; AP Photo/Armando Trovati, p. 25; STR/EPA/Newscom, p. 26; AP Photo/Pier Marco Tacca, p. 27.

Cover: GUILLAUME HORCAJUELO/EPA/Newscom (Lindsey Vonn); © iStockphoto.com/neyro2008 (motion lines); © iStockphoto.com/ulimi (black and white stars).